Pushing Up the Sky

PUSHING UP THE SKY

Seven Native American Plays for Children

✳ ✳ ✳ ✳

Joseph Bruchac
illustrated by Teresa Flavin

Center for the Collaborative Classroom

To my sister Margaret,
whose love of the theater has always inspired me J.B.

For Cory T. F.

᭝᭝᭝ ᭝᭝᭝ ᭝᭝᭝ ᭝᭝᭝ ᭝᭝᭝ ᭝᭝᭝ ᭝᭝᭝ ᭝᭝᭝ ᭝᭝᭝ ᭝᭝᭝ ᭝᭝᭝ ᭝᭝᭝ ᭝᭝᭝ ᭝᭝᭝ ᭝᭝᭝ ᭝᭝᭝ ᭝᭝᭝ ᭝᭝᭝ ᭝᭝᭝ ᭝᭝᭝

Text copyright © 2000 by Joseph Bruchac
Illustrations copyright © 2000 by Teresa Flavin
Designed by Nancy R. Leo-Kelly

*The artist would like to thank the staff of the Resource Center at
the National Museum of the American Indian for their help with her research.*

Center for the Collaborative Classroom
1001 Marina Village Parkway, Suite 110
Alameda, CA 94501
800.666.7270 ∗ fax: 510.464.3670
collaborativeclassroom.org

ISBN 978-1-61003-552-1
Printed in China

3 4 5 6 7 8 9 10 RRD 22 21 20 19 18 17

*The full-color artwork was rendered in gouache on colored drawing stock.
The black-and-white artwork was rendered in pen and ink.*

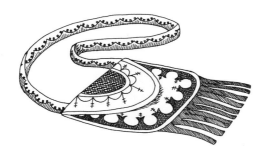

Author's Note

I hope young people putting on these plays, and the adults working with them, will be guided by the simple ideas I have provided for costuming and staging. The suggestions are appropriate for the Native people to whom each story belongs, and add to our understanding of the different tribal groups whose stories are retold in the plays.

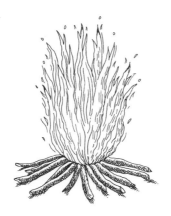

Contents

Pushing Up the Sky

Gluskabe and Old Man Winter

Abenaki

The homeland of the Abenaki people is the area now known as northern New England, where the winters can be very cold. The Abenakis lived in small villages near the rivers, which were their highways. Their birchbark-covered homes were called wigwams and were shaped like domes or large cones. Their seasonal round of life would find them fishing at the rivers or the seashore in the spring and summer, and hunting for deer, moose, and caribou in the woods in the autumn and winter. Their fields of corn, beans, squash, and other plants were grown in the river valleys and at the edges of the big lakes. Today many Abenaki people still live in Vermont, New Hampshire, and Maine, and Abenaki children still love to hear stories of Gluskabe's clever tricks.

Characters

SPEAKING ROLES:

NARRATOR

GLUSKABE

GRANDMOTHER WOODCHUCK

HUMAN BEING

OLD MAN WINTER

FOUR OR MORE SUMMER LAND PEOPLE, INCLUDING THE LEADER*

FOUR CROWS

*Note: Each of the four speaking parts for the Summer Land People can be spoken by several children at once if a large group is performing the play.

NON-SPEAKING ROLES:

SUN

FLOWERS

PLANTS

Props/Scenery

Gluskabe and Grandmother Woodchuck's wigwam can be made of folding chairs placed back to back a few feet apart and draped with white sheets or blankets decorated to look like birchbark with ∧-shaped marks cut from black construction paper. Shapes of ferns, half-moons, and stars can also be cut from construction paper and pinned to the sheets or blankets as decorations for the wigwams.

Old Man Winter's wigwam can be made by draping the same folding chairs with white sheets to look like snow.

Old Man Winter's fire made of ice can be suggested by a large ball of wax paper.

The Sun, Flowers, and Plants carry decorated paper cutouts.

Gluskabe's bag can be any large tote bag or sack.

Four balls each should be about the size of a child's head.

The pot full of summer is a large bowl that can be covered with red construction paper. Inside are the **summersticks:** several lighted flashlights, each wrapped in red paper or foil.

A rattle can be made by taping a pencil to a small milk carton covered with paper and filled with dried beans.

Costumes

Narrator carries a tote bag decorated with a fern design, representing a storyteller's bag (which, by tradition, would have held objects to remind the storyteller of the elements of his tale).

Gluskabe wears a red blanket or towel around his shoulders.

Grandmother Woodchuck wears a brown blanket.

Human Being wears a headband and leggings made of brown cloth.

Old Man Winter's white hair can be suggested with a wig made of cotton. He is dressed in white, with a white blanket or towel around his shoulders.

The Summer Land People wear eye patches, which can be made of felt circles sewed to a length of stretchy elastic. Make an extra eye patch to be worn by Gluskabe in Scene III.

The Crows wear black blankets or towels.

✳ ✳ ✳ ✳

Scene I: Gluskabe and Grandmother Woodchuck's Wigwam

Gluskabe and Grandmother Woodchuck sit inside with their blankets over their shoulders.

NARRATOR: Long ago Gluskabe (gloo-SKAH-bey) lived with his grandmother, Woodchuck, who was old and very wise. Gluskabe's job was to help the people.

GLUSKABE: It is very cold this winter, Grandmother.

GRANDMOTHER WOODCHUCK: *Ni ya yo* (nee yah yo), Grandson. You are right!

GLUSKABE: The snow is very deep, Grandmother.

GRANDMOTHER WOODCHUCK: *Ni ya yo,* Grandson.

GLUSKABE: It has been winter for a very long time, Grandmother.

GRANDMOTHER WOODCHUCK: *Ni ya yo,* Grandson. But look, here comes one of those human beings who are our friends.

HUMAN BEING: *Kwai, kwai, nidobak* (kwy kwy nee-DOH-bahk). Hello, my friends.

GLUSKABE AND GRANDMOTHER WOODCHUCK: *Kwai, kwai, nidoba* (kwy kwy nee-DOH-bah).

HUMAN BEING: Gluskabe, I have been sent by the other human beings to ask you for help. This winter has been too long. If it does not end soon, we will all die.

GLUSKABE: I will do what I can. I will go to the wigwam of Old Man Winter. He has stayed here too long. I will ask him to go back to his home in the Winter Land to the north.

GRANDMOTHER WOODCHUCK: Be careful, Gluskabe.

GLUSKABE: Don't worry, Grandmother. Winter cannot beat me.

Scene II: The Wigwam of Old Man Winter

Old Man Winter sits in his wigwam, "warming" his hands over his fire made of ice. The four balls of summer are on one side of the stage. Gluskabe enters stage carrying his bag and stands to the side of the wigwam door. He taps on the wigwam.

OLD MAN WINTER: Who is there!

GLUSKABE: It is Gluskabe.

OLD MAN WINTER: Ah, come inside and sit by my fire.

Gluskabe enters the wigwam.

GLUSKABE: The people are suffering. You must go back to your home in the Winter Land.

OLD MAN WINTER: Oh, I must, eh? But tell me, do you like my fire?

GLUSKABE: I do not like your fire. Your fire is not warm. It is cold.

OLD MAN WINTER: Yes, my fire is made of ice. And so are you!

Old Man Winter throws his white sheet over Gluskabe. Gluskabe falls down. Old Man Winter stands up.

OLD MAN WINTER: No one can defeat me!

Old Man Winter pulls Gluskabe out of the lodge. Then he goes back inside and closes the door flap. The Sun comes out and shines on Gluskabe. Gluskabe sits up and looks at the Sun.

GLUSKABE: Ah, that was a good nap! But I am not going into Old Man Winter's lodge again until I talk with my grandmother.

Gluskabe begins walking across the stage toward the four balls. Grandmother Woodchuck enters.

GRANDMOTHER WOODCHUCK: It is still winter, Gluskabe! Did Old Man Winter refuse to speak to you?

GLUSKABE: We spoke, but he did not listen. I will speak to him again; and I will make him listen. But tell me, Grandmother, where does the warm weather come from?

GRANDMOTHER WOODCHUCK: It is kept in the Summer Land.

GLUSKABE: I will go there and bring summer back here.

GRANDMOTHER WOODCHUCK: Grandson, the Summer Land people are strange people. Each of them has one eye. They are also greedy. They do not want to share the warm weather. It will be dangerous.

GLUSKABE: Why will it be dangerous?

GRANDMOTHER WOODCHUCK: The Summer Land people keep the summer in a big pot. They dance around it. Four giant crows guard the pot full of summer. Whenever a stranger tries to steal summer, those crows fly down and pull off his head!

GLUSKABE: Grandmother, I will go to the Summer Land. I will cover up one eye and look like the people there. And I will take these four balls of sinew with me.

Gluskabe picks up the four balls, places them in his bag, and puts the bag over his shoulder.

Scene III: The Summer Land Village

The Summer Land People are dancing around the pot full of summer. They are singing a snake dance song, following their leader, who shakes a rattle in one hand. Four Crows stand guard around the pot as the people dance.

SUMMER LAND PEOPLE: *Wee gai wah neh (wee guy wah ney),*

Wee gai wah neh,

Wee gai wah neh, wee gai wah neh,

Wee gai wah neh, wee gai wah neh,

Wee gai wah neh.

Gluskabe enters, wearing an eye patch and carrying his bag with the balls in it.

GLUSKABE: *Kwai, kwai, nidobak!* Hello, my friends.

Everyone stops dancing. They gather around Gluskabe.

LEADER OF THE SUMMER LAND PEOPLE: Who are you?

GLUSKABE: I am not a stranger. I am one of you. See, I have one eye.

SECOND SUMMER LAND PERSON: I do not remember you.

GLUSKABE: I have been gone a long time.

THIRD SUMMER LAND PERSON: He does have only one eye.

FOURTH SUMMER LAND PERSON: Let's welcome him back. Come join in our snake dance.

The singing and dancing begin again: "Wee gai wah neh," etc.
Gluskabe is at the end of the line as the dancers circle the pot full of
summer. When Gluskabe is close enough, he reaches in, grabs one of
the summersticks, and breaks away, running back and forth.

LEADER OF THE SUMMER LAND PEOPLE: He has taken one of our summersticks!

SECOND SUMMER LAND PERSON: Someone stop him!

THIRD SUMMER LAND PERSON: Crows, catch him!

FOURTH SUMMER LAND PERSON: Pull off his head!

The Crows swoop after Gluskabe. He reaches into his pouch and pulls out one of the balls. As each Crow comes up to him, he ducks his head down and holds up the ball. The Crow grabs the ball. Gluskabe keeps running, and pulls out another ball, repeating his actions until each of the Crows has grabbed a ball.

FIRST CROW: *Gah-gah!* I have his head.

SECOND CROW: *Gah-gah!* No, I have his head!

THIRD CROW: *Gah-gah!* Look, I have his head!

FOURTH CROW: *Gah-gah!* No, look—I have it too!

LEADER OF THE SUMMER LAND PEOPLE: How many heads did that stranger have?

SECOND SUMMER LAND PERSON: He has tricked us. He got away.

Scene IV: The Wigwam of Old Man Winter

Gluskabe walks up to Old Man Winter's wigwam. He holds the summerstick in his hand and taps on the door.

OLD MAN WINTER: Who is there!

GLUSKABE: It is Gluskabe.

OLD MAN WINTER: Ah, come inside and sit by my fire.

Gluskabe enters, sits down, and places the summerstick in front of Old Man Winter.

GLUSKABE: You must go back to your home in the Winter Land.

OLD MAN WINTER: Oh, I must, eh? But tell me, do you like my fire?

GLUSKABE: Your fire is no longer cold. It is getting warmer. Your wigwam is melting away. You are getting weaker.

OLD MAN WINTER: No one can defeat me!

GLUSKABE: Old Man, you are defeated. Warm weather has returned. Go back to your home in the north.

The blanket walls of Old Man Winter's wigwam collapse. Old Man Winter stands up and walks away as swiftly as he can, crouching down as if getting smaller. People carrying the cutouts of the Sun, Flowers, and Plants come out and surround Gluskabe as he sits there, smiling.

NARRATOR: So Gluskabe defeated Old Man Winter. Because he brought only one small piece of summer, winter still returns each year. But, thanks to Gluskabe, spring always comes back again.

Star Sisters

Ojibway

The Ojibway people, who are also known as the Chippewa, are one of the largest tribes in North America. The center of their homelands is the Great Lakes region of the present-day United States and Canada. Their lifestyle was much like that of their cousins, the Abenakis, who lived far to the east of them. The Ojibway people relied on their great knowledge of the forests and waters—not only hunting and fishing, but also making maple syrup, gathering berries, and traveling widely in their birchbark canoes.

Characters

NARRATOR

RED STAR SISTER

WHITE STAR SISTER

RED STAR

WHITE STAR

STAR PEOPLE (as many as the group size accommodates)

STAR GRANDMOTHER

LITTLE STAR

BEAR

LYNX

WOLVERINE

TREES (two or more)

Props/Scenery

Blankets are needed for Scene I.

The forest for Scene I can be suggested by a painted backdrop or potted plants.

A box or stepladder is needed for entrance of Red and White Stars in Scene I.

The Sky Land for Scene II can be suggested by a backdrop of dark paper covered with stars.

The holes in the sky for Scene III can be suggested by circles cut from black construction paper.

The basket for Scene III can be a large laundry basket decorated with gold stars.

The eagle's nest for Scene IV can be a child's inflatable pool or simply a painted backdrop suggesting part of the curving wall of the nest.

The kinnikinnick (dry willow bark) for Scene IV can be a handful of dried leaves or bark.

Costumes

Narrator wears a black T-shirt decorated with a gold star.

Red Star Sister wears a red T-shirt with sleeves "fringed" into strips to suggest buckskin.

White Star Sister wears a white T-shirt with fringed sleeves.

Red Star wears a red wig and fringed T-shirt with a red star on it.

White Star wears a white wig and a fringed T-shirt with a white star on it.

Star People each wear a fringed T-shirt (any color except black) decorated with a gold star.

Star Grandmother wears a white wig in addition to her "Star People" costume.

Little Star has the smallest gold star on his T-shirt.

Bear, Lynx, and Wolverine wear masks made from paper plates decorated with markers, yarn whiskers, etc. The mask can be held by hand in front of the wearer's face or mounted on a handle like a fan.

The Trees carry paper cutouts of trees.

✳ ✳ ✳ ✳

Scene I: A Forest at Night

Red Star Sister and White Star Sister lie on blankets outdoors in the forest.

NARRATOR: One night, two sisters went outside to sleep under the stars.

RED STAR SISTER: Look up into the sky.

WHITE STAR SISTER: It is beautiful up there.

RED STAR SISTER: I would like to marry a star.

WHITE STAR SISTER: I, too, would like to marry a star.

RED STAR SISTER: Which one would you marry?

WHITE STAR SISTER: I would marry that big white star.

RED STAR SISTER: I would marry that bright red star.

WHITE STAR SISTER: I am feeling very tired.

RED STAR SISTER: I am tired too.

The two Sisters fall asleep. As soon as they do so, Red Star and White Star enter. Their entry should suggest that they come from above the stage area, by jumping down onto the stage from a box or coming down a ladder.

RED STAR: This is my wife-to-be.

WHITE STAR: This is the one who wants to marry me.

RED STAR: Let us take them to the Sky Land now!

Scene II: The Sky Land

White Star Sister and Red Star Sister are asleep on the bare stage. They are surrounded by a crowd of Star People.

RED STAR SISTER *(waking)*: Where are we? Sister, wake up!

WHITE STAR SISTER: I dreamt that a star came down from the sky. Ah, who are these people?

ALL OF THE STAR PEOPLE: We are the Star People.

WHITE STAR SISTER: Sister, I am still dreaming. I want to wake up now and go back home.

STAR GRANDMOTHER: You are not dreaming.

LITTLE STAR: You are in the sky.

Red Star Sister and White Star Sister stand up.

RED STAR SISTER: How did we get up into the sky?

RED STAR: Do you not remember? You said you wanted to marry me. I am Red Star.

WHITE STAR: And your sister said she wanted to marry me. I am White Star.

WHITE STAR SISTER: Where is our wigwam?

LITTLE STAR *(pointing to floor)*: It is way down there.

STAR GRANDMOTHER: Every night our job is to look down through the holes in the sky.

ALL OF THE STAR PEOPLE: When people look up, they see our faces looking at them.

WHITE STAR *(taking White Star Sister's hand)*: Come with me, my wife. I will show you your new home.

RED STAR (*taking Red Star Sister's hand*): My wife, come with me. I will show you your new home too.

Scene III: Nighttime in Another Part of the Sky Land

White Star Sister and Red Star Sister are walking around the stage. The basket is on one side of the stage. All around them Star People are kneeling or lying on the stage with their faces looking down through the holes in the sky. As White Star Sister and Red Star Sister walk around, the Star People look up at them and then look back down again.

WHITE STAR SISTER: We have been in the sky for a long time, Sister.

RED STAR SISTER: Has White Star been kind to you?

WHITE STAR SISTER: He has been very kind to me, but there is nothing to do here in the Sky Land.

RED STAR SISTER: Red Star has been kind to me too. But I miss my home.

LITTLE STAR: Are you sad?

RED STAR SISTER: Yes, we are, Little Star.

LITTLE STAR: Why?

WHITE STAR SISTER: I miss my mother and father.

RED STAR SISTER: I miss my home and my friends.

LITTLE STAR: Come with me. I will take you to my grandmother.

Little Star leads the Star Sisters across the stage to Star Grandmother. Red Star and White Star are nearby, looking through holes in the sky.

LITTLE STAR: Grandmother, they are sad. They miss their families and their friends.

STAR GRANDMOTHER: Look down through this hole. What do you see?

RED STAR SISTER *(looking)*: I see my family's wigwam.

WHITE STAR SISTER *(looking)*: I can hear my people singing.

STAR GRANDMOTHER: You are ready to go home.

RED STAR *(standing up)*: If you are ready to go home, we will help you.

WHITE STAR *(also standing)*: We will miss you.

RED STAR: But you should be with your family.

STAR GRANDMOTHER: Get into this basket. We will tie a long rope to it.

The Star Sisters climb into the basket.

ALL OF THE STAR PEOPLE: We will lower you to the world below.

Scene IV: Eagle's Nest in the Forest

White Star Sister and Red Star Sister are standing in the nest, peering upward. The Trees stand in the background.

RED STAR SISTER: Wait, Star People! Do not take the basket away. We have not reached the ground yet. We are in an eagle's nest at the top of a tree.

WHITE STAR SISTER: They cannot hear you.

RED STAR SISTER: How can we get down from this treetop?

WHITE STAR SISTER: We will call for help. Look, there is Bear.

RED STAR SISTER: Come up here and help us get down.

BEAR: Who is asking me for help?

WHITE STAR SISTER: We are! Up here, in the eagle's nest!

BEAR: I am too busy to help you. I am looking for berries and honey.

RED STAR SISTER: He is going away. Oh, how can we get down?

WHITE STAR SISTER: Look, there is Lynx.

RED STAR SISTER: Please help us get down.

LYNX: Who wants help?

WHITE STAR SISTER: Here, up here.

LYNX: My claws are not sharp enough. That is too far to climb up.

RED STAR SISTER: He is going away too.

WHITE STAR SISTER: Who is that coming?

RED STAR SISTER: Oh no, it is Wolverine. If Wolverine helps us, he will make us live with him.

WOLVERINE: Did I hear someone speak my name? Ah, looook. Twoooo pretty sisters in a tree. I will help them get doooown.

RED STAR SISTER: Go away, we do not need any help.

WHITE STAR SISTER: Shh. Let him help us down. I have a plan.

Wolverine helps the Star Sisters climb out of the eagle's nest and down the tree.

WOLVERINE: There, I have helped you doooown. Now you can come and cooook my fooood and live with me.

WHITE STAR SISTER: Wait, I forgot my comb.

RED STAR SISTER: I forgot my comb too.

WHITE STAR SISTER: Please climb back up and get our combs.

WOLVERINE: The forest is thick here. Hoooow will I find yoooou when I come back doooown?

WHITE STAR SISTER: We will whistle to you.

WOLVERINE: Wait here for me. Don't forget toooo whistle when I get back.

RED STAR SISTER: He's gone. Now let's run away. This is the path to our village.

WHITE STAR SISTER: Wait. I have to ask the trees for help. *(Takes the kinnikinnick from her pouch.)* Trees, I am placing this *kinnikinnick* (kih-NEE-kin-nik) here on the ground for you as a gift. Help us. When Wolverine comes down, whistle to him.

TREES: We will help you, little ones.

WHITE STAR SISTER: Now let's run away!

WOLVERINE: I am back noooow. I could not find your coooombs. Sisters, where are yooooou? Whistle toooo me. *(A Tree whistles.)* There yoooou are. *(Another Tree whistles.)* Or are yoooou there? *(Trees whistle all around him.)* Oh noooo, they have tricked me. Now I have noooo one to coooook for me.

NARRATOR: So White Star Sister and Red Star Sister tricked Wolverine and came home safely. And from then on, they never again slept out at night under the stars.

Possum's Tail

Cherokee

The Cherokee people originally lived in the area now known as the states of Georgia, Tennessee, and North Carolina. Because they adapted so quickly to the European way of life, they became known as one of the "civilized tribes." However, long before the coming of Europeans they had a sophisticated form of government and lived in large, well-organized villages.

In the early 1800's many Cherokee people were forced to leave their homes and move to Indian Territory by traveling the infamous Trail of Tears. Today Cherokee people live all over the United States, but their two contemporary tribal governments are in Oklahoma and North Carolina. Wily, wise Rabbit is still their favorite trickster character.

Characters

NARRATOR

BEAR

RABBIT

TURTLE

RACCOON

POSSUM

OTTER

CRICKET

Note: If more children wish to take part in the play, other animals, such as Deer, Owl, Chipmunk, Squirrel, Beaver, or Fox, can be represented as non-speaking parts.

Props/Scenery

The forest can be suggested by a painted backdrop or potted plants.

A bandage is needed for Possum's tail.

A medicine bottle or **bowl** is also needed for Possum's tail.

The oak tree for Scene III can be painted on a backdrop.

Costumes

Narrator wears a turban made of patterned cloth.

Animal roles can be represented by masks made from paper plates decorated with markers, yarn, cotton balls, beads, etc. The mask can be held by hand in front of the wearer's face or mounted on a handle like a fan.

Possum's furry tail can be made of dark socks stuffed with cotton and stitched together.

Possum's rattail for Scene III can be a long piece of rope.

✳ ✳ ✳ ✳

Scene I: The Forest

A group of animals stands together.

NARRATOR: Long ago Possum had the most beautiful tail of all the animals. Everyone knew that was true. And if anyone didn't know, then Possum would tell him so.

BEAR: Tomorrow we will have a big meeting. Rabbit, you be the messenger. Go tell all the animals. We will meet at the big oak tree when Grandmother Sun rises up into the sky.

RABBIT: What will the meeting be about?

BEAR: We will decide that tomorrow.

TURTLE: Oh no, here comes Possum!

RACCOON: He is going to brag about his tail again. I can tell.

Possum enters and walks over to the other animals, holding his long tail in front of him.

POSSUM: *Siyo!* (see-yo) Hello! This day is beautiful. And so is my tail. Look at my beautiful tail.

OTHER ANIMALS: *Siyo,* Possum.

POSSUM: Did you say there would be a meeting tomorrow?

BEAR: Yes.

POSSUM: Then I should speak at the meeting.

TURTLE: Why?

OTTER: Turtle, don't ask him! He'll just talk about his—

POSSUM: Because of my beautiful tail. It is the most beautiful of all. It is not short like Bear's tail. It is long and silky. It is not stiff like Raccoon's tail. It is soft and lovely. It is not stubby like Rabbit's tail. It is fluffy and big. It is not ugly like Turtle's tail. It is pretty and nice. *(Possum can continue to improvise while Bear and Rabbit speak, saying "Isn't it beautiful?" etc.)*

As Possum goes on talking, the other animals yawn and roll their eyes. One by one they fall to the ground and pretend to sleep. During

this activity Rabbit taps Bear on the shoulder, and Rabbit and Bear step toward the audience. Possum does not notice, but keeps talking.

RABBIT: I have an idea about Possum.

BEAR: We should stuff moss into our ears so we cannot hear him?

RABBIT: No, I have a better idea than that. Let me whisper it to you.

Rabbit whispers into Bear's ear. Bear smiles and nods.

BEAR: That is a good idea.

Bear and Rabbit turn back toward Possum, who is still talking. The other animals are still pretending to sleep, but Possum doesn't notice.

RABBIT: Possum, you *do* have a beautiful tail.

POSSUM: Yes. That is true. Shall I tell you about it?

BEAR: No! I mean, not now.

RABBIT: We have decided that you should be the first speaker at the big meeting tomorrow.

POSSUM: Of course. That is true. The one with the most beautiful tail should always speak first.

RABBIT: Possum, your tail should look its best for the meeting.

POSSUM: Of course. That is true. My tail should look its best.

RABBIT: I will take you to Cricket. He will put some special medicine on your tail. Then your tail will be ready for the meeting.

POSSUM: Of course. That is true. Let us go to Cricket.

Possum and Rabbit go offstage together. The other animals open their eyes and sit up.

RACCOON: Oh, no!

OTTER: If Possum's tail is made more beautiful, he'll never stop talking.

TURTLE: Otter is right. We'll all have to move away to escape his bragging.

BEAR: Don't worry. Rabbit has a plan.

Scene II: Another Part of the Forest

Cricket crouches on the ground.

RABBIT: Cricket, I want you to put some of your *special* medicine on Possum's tail.

POSSUM: Yes. That is true. I want my tail to look even more beautiful.

CRICKET: Rabbit, do you mean my *special* medicine?

RABBIT: Yes, I mean your *special* medicine.

POSSUM: Hurry up. I want you to fix my tail.

CRICKET: I will fix it. *(Cricket pretends to apply medicine to Possum's tail from either a bottle or a bowl.)* This medicine will make your tail look as it has never looked before.

POSSUM: Will everyone notice it?

CRICKET: Oh yes, everyone will notice it. *(Cricket wraps a bandage around Possum's tail.)* Now you must keep this old snakeskin wrapped around your tail all night. Do not take it off until you are at the meeting.

Scene III: The Forest, Near the Big Oak Tree

All the animals are gathered in a semicircle. Possum's tail is still wrapped in the snakeskin.

BEAR: Possum will open our meeting.

RABBIT: Everyone, pay attention.

POSSUM: *Siyo,* everyone. I have been asked to speak today because of my tail. It is the most beautiful of all. Here, let me show you how beautiful it is.

Possum unwraps his tail. It now looks like a big rat's tail, but Possum does not notice.

RACCOON: Look at Possum's tail!

POSSUM (*still showing off the tail without looking at it*)**:** Yes. Look at my tail. Look at how beautiful it is.

TURTLE: It has no hair at all!

OTTER: It is really ugly.

RACCOON: It is funny looking.

The animals begin to laugh. Possum looks at his tail and sees that it has no hair.

POSSUM: My tail! Cricket has ruined it!

Possum sits down on the ground, closes his eyes, and then rolls onto his back with his feet up in the air. He stays there until all the other animals have gone. Then he gets up and runs away.

NARRATOR: So it is that Possum now has the ugliest tail of all the animals. Ever since that time, whenever Possum meets another animal, he closes his eyes, rolls over on his back, and pretends to be dead until the other animal goes away. And Possum no longer brags about his tail!

Wihio's Duck Dance

Cheyenne

The Cheyenne people originally lived in the area just west
of the Great Lakes, where they were farmers. With the coming of the horse the Cheyenne moved out onto the Great
Plains and soon became widely known as great buffalo
hunters. They followed the herds, dragging their belongings
on poles behind their horses and setting up tall tipis covered
with buffalo skins. They were regarded as a very brave and
honorable people, never many in number but fierce in the
defense of their people. Today the Cheyenne nation is split
into the Northern Cheyenne in Montana and the Southern
Cheyenne in Oklahoma. Their trickster hero, Wihio, is
much like the trickster heroes of their neighbors, the
Ojibway and Lakotas. Wihio is clever, but so greedy and
foolish that he usually ends up losing in the end. Cheyenne
children are still told: "Don't be like Wihio!"

Characters

NARRATOR

WIHIO

FIRST DUCK

SECOND DUCK

THIRD DUCK

FOURTH DUCK

FIFTH DUCK

OTHER DUCKS (as many as group size will accommodate)

TREE

COYOTE

Props/Scenery

The lake for Scene I can be suggested by a blue rug or blanket on the stage.

The interior of Wihio's lodge can be suggested with a painted back-drop showing poles in a tipi shape covered by dark skins.

The outside of Wihio's lodge can be suggested by a painting of a large tipi on a backdrop. Pictures of buffalo and horses can be drawn on the lodge.

The drum can be a real drum or an upside-down wastebasket.

The fires for Scenes II and III can be suggested by crumpled sheets of red, yellow, and orange tissue or construction paper surrounded by a ring of stones.

Two ducks caught by Wihio can be made of paper or can be stuffed toys.

Costumes

Narrator wears a blanket draped from right shoulder to left hip and fastened at the waist with a leather belt.

Wihio wears a brown "fringed" T-shirt and brown leggings, which can be made of cloth.

Ducks wear decorated masks made of paper plates, with duck beaks sticking out in front.

The Tree holds two dead tree branches, one in each hand.

Coyote wears a tail and ears made of tan or gray felt; the ears can be sewn to a headband and the tail pinned to the back of clothing.

✳ ✳ ✳ ✳

Scene I: A Lake

The Ducks walk in circles on the lake, flapping their elbows as if swimming.

NARRATOR: One day Wihio (Wee-HE-yo) was out walking around. He was feeling as if hunger had cut him in half. Then he saw some ducks on a lake, and he had an idea for a way to get himself some roasted duck to eat.

WIHIO: Ducks love to dance. I will have a special duck dance for my friends. Hey, all you ducks, come to my lodge! I am having a dance.

Wihio walks offstage.

FIRST DUCK: Wihio is going to have a dance for us.

SECOND DUCK: Should we go?

THIRD DUCK: Wihio likes to trick people.

FOURTH DUCK: Wihio can be dangerous.

FIFTH DUCK: But I love to dance.

FIRST DUCK: I love to dance too.

FIFTH DUCK: Let's go to Wihio's duck dance.

ALL DUCKS: Yes, let's go.

Scene II: Inside Wihio's Lodge

Wihio sits near the front of the stage, a big drum in front of him. There is a fire in the center of the stage. The Ducks enter the lodge one by one through an imaginary door flap.

WIHIO: Welcome to my lodge, friends.

ALL DUCKS: Thank you, Wihio.

WIHIO: Now we will have a special duck dance. I will play the drum. To do this dance you must dance around the fire in a circle with your eyes shut. If you open your eyes, they will turn red from the smoke.

ALL DUCKS: We will keep our eyes shut.

WIHIO: Good. Now dance!

Wihio plays the drum as the Ducks start to dance in a circle, moving counterclockwise around the fire. As Wihio plays, he shouts out the word "Hey" on every seventh beat.

WIHIO: (BOOM-BOOM

BOOM-BOOM

BOOM-BOOM)

HEY!

Wihio repeats his drumming as the Ducks talk.

FIRST DUCK: This is a good dance.

THIRD DUCK: It is fun after all.

FIFTH DUCK: I love to dance!

WIHIO: Keep dancing. Keep your eyes shut.

(BOOM-BOOM

 BOOM-BOOM

 BOOM-BOOM)

 HEY!

As the Ducks move in their circle, they must dance close to Wihio. When First Duck dances past, Wihio reaches out and grabs the Duck as he shouts "HEY," yanking it out of the circle to stand next to him. First Duck also shouts "HEY" when it is grabbed, but the other Ducks do not seem to notice. Wihio captures Second Duck the same way, and continues catching Ducks until Fourth Duck opens his eyes.

FOURTH DUCK: First Duck, did you hear something?

FIFTH DUCK: I love to dance!

FOURTH DUCK: First Duck, answer me. Where is First Duck? I am going to open my eyes. WAAAACK, WIHIO IS GRABBING US. FLY AWAY. FLY AWAY!

All of the Ducks run for the door of the lodge, knocking Wihio over as they fly away. Even the Ducks Wihio has already caught get up and run away. When he stands up again, he is holding two toy ducks, one in each hand. He runs out the door and offstage, holding up his ducks triumphantly.

Scene III: Outside Wihio's Lodge

Wihio enters holding the two toy ducks in his hands. He goes over to the cooking fire, which is near the Tree.

WIHIO: Those other ducks were too little and skinny to eat. I have caught the two biggest ones. Now I will have a feast.

Wihio places the two toy ducks into the fire to cook them.

WIHIO: They will be cooked soon. I am so hungry.

The Tree begins making squeaking noises with its mouth while rubbing its branches together.

TREE: SQUEAK, SQUEAAAAK.

WIHIO: What is that awful noise?

TREE: SQUEAK, SQUEAAAAK.

WIHIO: If you don't stop, I will climb up there and stop you.

TREE: SQUEAK, SQUEAAAAK.

WIHIO: I warned you.

Wihio stands up, goes over to the Tree, and pantomines climbing it. He tries to push the branches apart and does so with great effort, but then the Tree closes its branches to trap Wihio.

WIHIO: Let go of me!

As Wihio struggles, Coyote walks onto the stage.

COYOTE: Do I smell food cooking?

WIHIO: Oh no. If Coyote finds my food, he will eat it. Coyote!

COYOTE: Wihio, what do you want?

WIHIO: Coyote, don't come over here.

COYOTE: Why not?

WIHIO: If you come over here, you will find my food and eat it.

COYOTE: Over where?

WIHIO: Over here.

Coyote comes over to the fire.

WIHIO: No, no. Go away!

Coyote pulls out the two ducks and pantomimes eating them. Then he walks away, smiling and rubbing his stomach.

COYOTE: Thank you, Wihio! That was a good meal.

NARRATOR: So Wihio did not get to eat the ducks that he caught. He stayed in the tree until the wind blew those branches apart and he fell to the ground.

The Tree moves its branches apart, freeing Wihio.

WIHIO: Whooops! *(Falls to ground and picks himself up. Then he looks into the fire, but his food is all gone.)* Those ducks were too bony and skinny to eat anyway. *(Wihio walks away.)*

NARRATOR: So Wihio stayed hungry. And what about that little duck that opened its eyes during Wihio's dance and saved the others? That little duck is the one we call the coot. Ever since then, all coots have red eyes. And Wihio is still hungry.

Pushing Up the Sky

Snohomish

The Snohomish people live in the area of the Northwest that is now known as the state of Washington, not far from Puget Sound. They fished in the ocean and gathered food from the shore. Their homes and many of the things they used every day, such as bowls and canoe paddles, were carved from the trees. Like many of the other peoples of the area, they also carved totem poles, which recorded the history and stories of their nation. This story is one that was carved into a totem pole made for the city of Everett, Washington, by Chief William Shelton.

Characters

SPEAKING ROLES:

NARRATOR

TALL MAN

GIRL

MOTHER

BOY

FIRST CHIEF

SECOND CHIEF

THIRD CHIEF

FOURTH CHIEF

FIFTH CHIEF

SIXTH CHIEF

SEVENTH CHIEF

NON-SPEAKING ROLES:

Animals and Birds—as many as group size will accommodate. Animals familiar to the Snohomish would include Dog, Deer, Elk, Mountain Goat, Bear, Mountain Lion, Rabbit, Weasel, Wolf, and Fox. Birds would include Hawk, Bald Eagle, Golden Eagle, Jay, Seagull, Raven, Heron, and Kingfisher.

Props/Scenery

The village can be suggested with a painted backdrop showing houses made of cedar planks among tall fir trees and redwoods, with the ocean visible in the background. Potted plants can be added around the stage to suggest trees if desired.

Bows and arrows held by Boy in Scene I can be from a toy set or made from cardboard.

The poles held by people and animals in Scene III can be rulers or long tubes of cardboard.

Costumes

People, including the **Narrator**, can wear blankets or towels. **Chiefs** wear them around their shoulders, and other humans wear them wrapped around their waists to suggest the robes often worn by people of the Northwest. Cone-shaped hats (worn by Snohomish women) may be worn by girls playing human characters.

Depending on their number and type, the **Animals** can be suggested by face paint or with decorated masks made from paper plates.

✳ ✳ ✳ ✳

Scene I: A Village Among Many Tall Trees

Tall Man, Girl, Mother, and Boy stand onstage.

NARRATOR: Long ago the sky was very close to the earth. The sky was so close that some people could jump right into it. Those people who were not good jumpers could climb up the tall fir trees and step into the sky. But people were not happy that the sky was so close to the earth. Tall people kept bumping their heads on the sky. And there were other problems.

TALL MAN: Oh, that hurt! I just hit my head on the sky again.

GIRL: I just threw my ball and it landed in the sky and I can't get it back.

MOTHER: Where is my son? Has he climbed a tree and gone up into the sky again?

BOY: Every time I shoot my bow, my arrows get stuck in the sky!

ALL: THE SKY IS TOO CLOSE!

Scene II: The Same Village

The seven chiefs stand together onstage.

NARRATOR: So people decided something had to be done. A great meeting was held for all the different tribes. The seven wisest chiefs got together to talk about the problem.

FIRST CHIEF: My people all think the sky is too close.

SECOND CHIEF: The Creator did a very good job of making the world.

THIRD CHIEF: That is true, but the Creator should have put the sky up higher. My tall son keeps hitting his head on the sky.

FOURTH CHIEF: My daughter keeps losing her ball in the sky.

FIFTH CHIEF: People keep going up into the sky when they should be staying on the earth to help each other.

SIXTH CHIEF: When mothers look for their children, they cannot find them because they are up playing in the sky.

SEVENTH CHIEF: We are agreed, then. The sky is too close.

ALL: WE ARE AGREED.

SECOND CHIEF: What can we do?

SEVENTH CHIEF: I have an idea. Let's push up the sky.

THIRD CHIEF: The sky is heavy.

SEVENTH CHIEF: If we all push together, we can do it.

SIXTH CHIEF: We will ask the birds and animals to help. They also do not like it that the sky is so close.

SECOND CHIEF: The elk are always getting their antlers caught in the sky.

FOURTH CHIEF: The birds are always hitting their wings on it.

FIRST CHIEF: We will cut tall trees to make poles. We can use those poles to push up the sky.

FIFTH CHIEF: That is a good idea. Are we all agreed?

ALL: WE ARE ALL AGREED.

Scene III: The Same Village

All the People, except Seventh Chief, are gathered together. They hold long poles. The Birds and Animals are with them. They all begin pushing randomly, jabbing their poles into the air. (The sky can be imagined as just above them.)

GIRL: It isn't working!

BOY: The sky is still too close.

FIFTH CHIEF: Where is Seventh Chief? This was his idea!

SEVENTH CHIEF *(entering)***:** Here I am. I had to find this long pole.

FIRST CHIEF: Your plan is not good! See, we are pushing and the sky is not moving.

SEVENTH CHIEF: Ah, but I said we must push together.

FIFTH CHIEF: We need a signal so that all can push together. Our people speak different languages.

SEVENTH CHIEF: Let us use YAH-HOO as the signal. Ready?

ALL: YES!

SEVENTH CHIEF: YAH-HOO.

At the signal, everyone pushes together.

ALL: YAH-HOO!

SEVENTH CHIEF: YAH-HOO.

Again everyone pushes together.

ALL: YAH-HOO!

TALL MAN: We are doing it!

MOTHER: Now my son won't be able to hide in the sky!

SEVENTH CHIEF: YAH-HOO.

Again everyone pushes together.

ALL: YAH-HOO!

BOY: It will be too high for my arrows to stick into it.

SEVENTH CHIEF: YAH-HOO.

Again everyone pushes together.

ALL: YAH-HOOOO!

FIRST CHIEF: We have done it!

NARRATOR: So the sky was pushed up. It was done by everyone working together. That night, though, when everyone looked overhead, they saw many stars in the sky. The stars were shining through the holes poked into the sky by the poles of everyone who pushed it up higher.

No one ever bumped his head on the sky again. And those stars are there to this day.

The Cannibal Monster

Tlingit

The Tlingit (KLING-it) people live in the far north along the coast of Alaska. Dwelling in a land where woodlands and wildlife were abundant, they developed a culture rich in decorative arts, particularly wood carving. They carved giant canoes out of redwood trees and traveled great distances in them. They went out to sea to catch salmon and even hunt for whales. They built huge longhouses made of cedar planks, and carved and painted designs that stood for the animals of the land and the ocean on the doors and walls. They believed in sharing things with each other and often had great ceremonies called potlatches. At the potlatch, important people such as chiefs would give away many gifts to everyone.

The Tlingit are still great fishermen to this day and tell many stories of how things came to be. The Tlingit people also continue to make very tall totem poles that tell stories. Raven is usually carved on top of the pole. This story of the cannibal monster can be seen carved into a beautiful totem pole that stands on the campus of the University of Alaska in Fairbanks.

Characters

SPEAKING ROLES:

RAVEN

VILLAGE CHIEF

FIRST MAN

FIRST WOMAN

SECOND MAN

SECOND WOMAN

CANNIBAL MONSTER

BROWN BEAR

THIRD MAN

THIRD WOMAN

NON-SPEAKING ROLES:

OTHER PEOPLE—AS MANY AS GROUP SIZE WILL ACCOMMODATE

DRUMMER (offstage)

Props/Scenery

The **Tlingit village** can be suggested with a painted backdrop showing a large longhouse decorated with traditional Tlingit designs. Alternatively, children can paint large cardboard boxes to represent the longhouses.

Raven's tree can be represented with a painted backdrop. Raven can stand on a small **stepstool.**

A **drum** is needed to make the booming sound of the cannibal monster's approach. This can be a real drum or an upside-down wastebasket.

Spear for Brown Bear can be a child's toy (rubber, preferably) or made from a long cardboard tube with a cardboard spearhead.

The fire for Scene III can be created by placing a red sheet or large piece of paper with flames painted on it over the cannibal monster. Moving the sheet or the paper can create the impression of rippling flames.

Costumes

Raven dresses in black and wears a black mask fastened with elastic. In keeping with the design of traditional Tlingit masks, the mask ends above the actor's mouth, the beak overhanging his nose.

Village Chief wears a decorated and fringed blanket or sheet around his shoulders like a cape. The cape can be decorated with designs for one of the Tlingit clans. Designs of the different clans include the killer whale, the salmon, or the bear. (Be sure not to mix clan designs on the same person's clothing.) The chief wears a cone-shaped hat.

People wear everyday clothing with blankets or sheets wrapped around their waists. The blankets or sheets should be decorated with the designs of one clan or another. All people wear cone-shaped hats.

Cannibal Monster can be carried by two children hidden inside its costume. The monster can be made of sheets hung over a tall pole with a cross pole at the top. The head, which can be made of painted papier-mâché, should be as large as possible, with a long nose and a big mouth. Fasten it to the top of the pole. Be sure to cut holes in the sheets so the children inside can look out.

Brown Bear (who is human, not an animal) wears blankets or sheets decorated with bear designs. Brown Bear also wears a cone-shaped hat.

✳ ✳ ✳ ✳

Scene I: A Village on the Northwest Coast

The people of the village pantomime various activities such as carving wood, fixing fishing nets, working on canoes, and mixing food. Raven stands in his tree to one side of the stage.

RAVEN: Caa-awk, caa-awk. My name is Raven. One of my jobs is to keep watch. That's why you see me on top of the tallest trees like this one. I can see better up here. Let me tell you a story about something I saw once long ago. It's a good story. It's about a monster and some brave people. It's a story about me too. Caa-awk, caa-awk! That makes the story even better.

VILLAGE CHIEF: What a good day this is. I am glad we moved to this village.

FIRST MAN: I just hope that the cannibal monster does not find us again.

Offstage, Drummer beats the drum, BOOM-BOOM-BOOM-BOOM, like heavy feet striking the earth.

FIRST WOMAN: Oh no, do you hear that sound?

SECOND MAN: I think it is the cannibal monster!

VILLAGE CHIEF: Maybe it is just the sound of thunder.

SECOND MAN: Or rocks rolling down the mountain.

Offstage, Drummer makes the BOOM-BOOM-BOOM-BOOM sound again, louder this time. Then Cannibal Monster gives a loud ROAR.

SECOND WOMAN: It is the cannibal monster. Run for your lives!

The people run in all directions as Cannibal Monster enters the village.

CANNIBAL MONSTER: WEY-HAH! I AM HUNGRY!

BROWN BEAR: Throw your spears at it. Shoot your arrows.

The people pantomime throwing spears and shooting arrows.

CANNIBAL MONSTER: WEY-HAH! SPEARS AND ARROWS CANNOT HURT ME!

The cannibal monster turns to chase First Man offstage.

FIRST MAN *(from offstage)*: Help! The cannibal monster is going to catch me! Agggghhh!

RAVEN: As you can see, things were not going well for the human beings. Luckily for them, I decided to help.

Scene II: The Same Village

Brown Bear sits alone in the village. Raven is in his tree above him.

BROWN BEAR: What can we do? Nothing can kill that monster.

RAVEN: Caa-awk, caa-awk. I can help. I can help.

BROWN BEAR: Raven, how can you help us? Do you know how to kill the cannibal monster?

RAVEN: Shoot the monster in its left heel. Shoot the monster in its left heel.

BROWN BEAR: I will do as you say, Raven. Thank you.

Scene III: The Same Village

People are gathered around Brown Bear.

VILLAGE CHIEF: Brown Bear, are you sure you know how to kill the cannibal monster?

BROWN BEAR: Raven told me. He wants to help us.

SECOND WOMAN: Remember what happened yesterday? Our spears didn't hurt the monster.

BROWN BEAR: It will be different today.

Offstage, Drummer makes BOOM-BOOM-BOOM-BOOM sound.

THIRD MAN: What is that?

THIRD WOMAN: It is the cannibal monster. Run for your lives!

BROWN BEAR: No. Everyone stay right here.

Cannibal Monster makes its ROAR sound offstage. Then monster enters.

CANNIBAL MONSTER: WEY-HAH! I AM HUNGRY.

BROWN BEAR: Try to eat me!

Brown Bear holds up his spear.

CANNIBAL MONSTER: WEY-HAH! YOU CANNOT HURT ME.

Cannibal Monster moves toward Brown Bear. Brown Bear ducks behind Cannibal Monster and stabs down with his spear at the monster's left heel.

CANNIBAL MONSTER: YOU HAVE KILLED ME!

Cannibal Monster falls down onto the stage.

VILLAGE CHIEF: It is dead.

FIRST WOMAN: Brown Bear has saved us all from being eaten alive.

THIRD MAN: But what can we do with the cannibal monster's body?

SECOND WOMAN: Let's burn it up!

RAVEN *(calling down from his tree)*: Caa-awk. Caa-awk. Bad idea. Bad idea.

VILLAGE CHIEF: That is a good idea. Everyone go get wood.

BROWN BEAR: Wait! Raven says that is a bad idea.

No one listens to Brown Bear. They all gather wood and pile it around Cannibal Monster's body.

RAVEN: Don't do it. Don't do it.

BROWN BEAR: Raven says we should not do this.

SECOND MAN: Brown Bear, step back. We are going to light the fire.

The People place the sheet of "fire" over Cannibal Monster.

RAVEN: You'll be sorry. You'll be sorry.

CANNIBAL MONSTER'S VOICE: YOU HAVE SET ME FREE. NOW I WILL EAT YOU FOREVER. WEY-HAH.WEY-HAH!

VILLAGE CHIEF *(swatting at something in the air)***:** Something is coming out of the smoke.

SECOND WOMAN: The smoke is turning into little creatures.

She swats her arm.

THIRD WOMAN: Ouch. One of them bit me!

Everyone is now swatting at the air and at their arms, legs, and heads.

FIRST WOMAN: They are eating us alive.

VLLAGE CHIEF: Run for your lives!

Everyone runs offstage, leaving Raven alone in his tree.

RAVEN: Caa-awk, caa-awk. They should have listened to me. That is how mosquitoes came into the world. They came out of the smoke from the cannibal monster's body. They are still eating people alive to this day. Caa-awk, caa-awk! And that is my story.

The Strongest One

Zuni

The Zunis are one of the peoples of the Southwest who dwell in pueblos, compact villages made up of multistoried buildings of adobe brick and beams. The Zunis' pueblo, which is also called Zuni, is located in present-day New Mexico. The Zunis and the other pueblo people developed means of growing their crops in the dry lands of the Southwest and are regarded as very sophisticated farmers.

The Zuni people are famous for their ceremonies, which are designed to give thanks and support to all living things, from the largest to the smallest. The Zunis are also very well-known as artists for their beautiful jewelry made of silver and turquoise.

Characters

NARRATOR

LITTLE RED ANT

SECOND ANT

THIRD ANT

FOURTH ANT

SNOW

SUN

WIND

HOUSE

MOUSE

CAT

STICK

FIRE

WATER

DEER

ARROW

BIG ROCK

Note: For a large group, children can share the parts of the Second, Third, and Fourth Ants. In a smaller group, one child can play several of the parts in Scene II.

Props/Scenery

Flashlights can be used for dim lighting in Scenes I and III.

The Mesa in Scene II can be suggested with a painted backdrop.

Costumes

Narrator wears a loose, flowing shirt over pants, with a silver necklace and a long head scarf tied at the side.

The Ants wear red T-shirts and red face paint. Their feelers can be suggested by securing red pipe cleaners around a child's headband.

Snow, Sun, Wind, Stick, Fire, Water, Big Rock all wear T-shirts decorated with their symbol (this can be drawn on paper and pinned to the T-shirt): snowflake, sun, wind with puffing cheeks, branch, flame, drop of water, boulder. Face paint can also be used.

House carries a large paper cutout depicting an adobe.

Mouse, Cat, Deer can be suggested with face paint, felt tails, and felt ears (or, for Deer, pipe-cleaner antlers) secured to a child's headband.

Arrow carries a large cardboard arrow.

✳ ✳ ✳ ✳

Scene I: Inside the Ants' Hole

On a darkened stage, the ants crouch together.

NARRATOR: Little Red Ant lived in a hole under the Big Rock with all of its relatives. It often wondered about the world outside: Who in the world was the strongest one of all? One day in late spring Little Red Ant decided to find out.

LITTLE RED ANT: I am going to find out who is strongest. I am going to go outside and walk around.

SECOND ANT: Be careful! We ants are very small. Something might step on you.

THIRD ANT: Yes, we are the smallest and weakest ones of all.

FOURTH ANT: Be careful, it is dangerous out there!

LITTLE RED ANT: I will be careful. I will find out who is strongest. Maybe the strongest one can teach us how to be stronger.

Scene II: The Mesa

Ant walks back and forth onstage.

NARRATOR: So Little Red Ant went outside and began to walk around. But as Little Red Ant walked, the snow began to fall.

Snow walks onstage.

LITTLE RED ANT: Ah, my feet are cold. This snow makes everything freeze. Snow must be the strongest. I will ask. Snow, are you the strongest of all?

SNOW: No, I am not the strongest.

LITTLE RED ANT: Who is stronger than you?

SNOW: Sun is stronger. When Sun shines on me, I melt away. Here it comes!

As Sun walks onstage, Snow hurries offstage.

LITTLE RED ANT: Ah, Sun must be the strongest. I will ask. Sun, are you the strongest of all?

SUN: No, I am not the strongest.

LITTLE RED ANT: Who is stronger than you?

SUN: Wind is stronger. Wind blows the clouds across the sky and covers my face. Here it comes!

As Wind comes onstage, Sun hurries offstage with face covered in hands.

LITTLE RED ANT: Wind must be the strongest. I will ask. Wind, are you the strongest of all?

WIND: No, I am not the strongest.

LITTLE RED ANT: Who is stronger than you?

WIND: House is stronger. When I come to House, I cannot move it. I must go elsewhere. Here it comes!

As House walks onstage, Wind hurries offstage.

LITTLE RED ANT: House must be the strongest. I will ask. House, are you the strongest of all?

HOUSE: No, I am not the strongest.

LITTLE RED ANT: Who is stronger than you?

HOUSE: Mouse is stronger. Mouse comes and gnaws holes in me. Here it comes!

As Mouse walks onstage, House hurries offstage.

LITTLE RED ANT: Mouse must be the strongest. I will ask. Mouse, are you the strongest of all?

MOUSE: No, I am not the strongest.

LITTLE RED ANT: Who is stronger than you?

MOUSE: Cat is stronger. Cat chases me, and if Cat catches me, Cat will eat me. Here it comes!

As Cat walks onstage, Mouse hurries offstage, squeaking.

LITTLE RED ANT: Cat must be the strongest. I will ask. Cat, are you the strongest of all?

CAT: No, I am not the strongest.

LITTLE RED ANT: Who is stronger than you?

CAT: Stick is stronger. When Stick hits me, I run away. Here it comes!

As Stick walks onstage, Cat hurries offstage, meowing.

LITTLE RED ANT: Stick must be the strongest. I will ask. Stick, are you the strongest of all?

STICK: No, I am not the strongest.

LITTLE RED ANT: Who is stronger than you?

STICK: Fire is stronger. When I am put into Fire, Fire burns me up! Here it comes!

As Fire walks onstage, Stick hurries offstage.

LITTLE RED ANT: Fire must be the strongest. I will ask. Fire, are you the strongest of all?

FIRE: No, I am not the strongest.

LITTLE RED ANT: Who is stronger than you?

FIRE: Water is stronger. When Water is poured on me, it kills me. Here it comes!

As Water walks onstage, Fire hurries offstage.

LITTLE RED ANT: Water must be the strongest. I will ask. Water, are you the strongest of all?

WATER: No, I am not the strongest.

LITTLE RED ANT: Who is stronger than you?

WATER: Deer is stronger. When Deer comes, Deer drinks me. Here it comes!

As Deer walks onstage, Water hurries offstage.

LITTLE RED ANT: Deer must be the strongest. I will ask. Deer, are you the strongest of all?

DEER: No, I am not the strongest.

LITTLE RED ANT: Who is stronger than you?

DEER: Arrow is stronger. When Arrow strikes me, it can kill me. Here it comes!

As Arrow walks onstage, Deer runs offstage with leaping bounds.

LITTLE RED ANT: Arrow must be the strongest. I will ask. Arrow, are you the strongest of all?

ARROW: No, I am not the strongest.

LITTLE RED ANT: Who is stronger than you?

ARROW: Big Rock is stronger. When I am shot from the bow and I hit Big Rock, Big Rock breaks me.

LITTLE RED ANT: Do you mean the same Big Rock where the Red Ants live?

ARROW: Yes, that is Big Rock. Here it comes!

As Big Rock walks onstage, Arrow runs offstage.

LITTLE RED ANT: Big Rock must be the strongest. I will ask. Big Rock, are you the strongest of all?

BIG ROCK: No, I am not the strongest.

LITTLE RED ANT: Who is stronger than you?

BIG ROCK: You are stronger. Every day you and the other Red Ants come and carry little pieces of me away. Someday I will be all gone.

Scene III: The Ants' Hole

NARRATOR: So Little Red Ant went back home and spoke to the ant people.

The ants crouch together on the darkened stage.

SECOND ANT: Little Red Ant has returned.

THIRD ANT: He has come back alive!

FOURTH ANT: Tell us about what you have learned. Who is the strongest of all?

LITTLE RED ANT: I have learned that everything is stronger than something else. And even though we ants are small, in some ways *we* are the strongest of all.

Sources/Bibliography

Gluskabe and Old Man Winter is adapted from my own version of the traditional Abenaki story as told in *The Wind Eagle* by Joseph Bruchac (Greenfield Center, N.Y.: Greenfield Review Press, 1986). Other reading: "Penobscot Tales and Religious Beliefs" by Frank Speck (*Journal of American Folklore,* Vol. 48, 1935); *The Algonquin Legends of New England* by Charles Godfrey Leland (Boston: Houghton Mifflin and Co., 1884).

Star Sisters is adapted, in part, from the story collected by Frank Speck in "Myths and Folklore of the Timiskaming Algonquin and Timigami Ojibway" in *GS Canada,* IX, Ottawa, 1915. Other reading: Stith Thompson's *Tales of the North American Indians* (Bloomington, Indiana: Indiana University Press, 1929, 1966).

Possum's Tail is adapted, in part, from the story collected by James Mooney in *Myths of the Cherokee,* Annual Report of the Bureau of American Ethnology, Washington, D.C., 1900. Other reading: *How Rabbit Tricked Otter* by Gayle Ross (New York: Harper Collins, 1994); *Friends of Thunder* by Anna and Jack Kilpatrick (Dallas, Texas: Southern Methodist University Press, 1961).

Wihio's Duck Dance is a story told throughout the Great Lakes and Northern Plains. A Cheyenne friend, writer Lance Henson, first told me about Wihio and his exploits a number of years ago, and Lakota storyteller Kevin Locke shared the Lakota version of this story with me. Other reading: *By Cheyenne Campfires* by George Bird Grinnell (New Haven, Connecticut: Yale University Press, 1926) contains a version of this tale entitled "Wihio and Coyote."

Pushing Up the Sky is adapted from the tale told by Chief William Shelton in *The Story of the Totem Pole* (self-published in Everett, Washington, 1935). Other reading: *Indian Legends of the Pacific Northwest* by Ella E. Clark (Berkeley, California: University of California Press, 1953).

The Cannibal Monster is one of the most widely told tales in North America. This version is adapted from the story told to me in Alaska by Tlingit author and oral historian Nora Dauenhauer. Other reading: *American Indian Myths and Legends* selected and edited by Richard Erdoes and Alfonso Ortiz (New York: Pantheon, 1985) contains a version of the Tlingit story titled "How Mosquitoes Came to Be," which leaves out mention of Raven. *The Legend of the Windigo* by Gayle Ross (New York: Dial Books for Young Readers, 1996) contains a retelling of the Cree story of the cannibal monster.

The Strongest One is adapted from a traditional Zuni story told to children in *Zuni Folk Tales,* collected by Frank H. Cushing (New York: G. P. Putnam's Sons, 1901). Other reading: *The Zuni: Self-Portrayals* by the Zuni People (Albuquerque, New Mexico: University of New Mexico Press, 1972).

JOSEPH BRUCHAC

is the author of over sixty acclaimed books for children and adults, many of which draw on the Native American culture that is part of his heritage. His retellings of traditional Native tales for Dial include *The First Strawberries: A Cherokee Story,* a 1994 Notable Children's Trade Book in the Field of Social Studies; *The Great Ball Game: A Muskogee Story,* a Child Study Children's Book of the Year; and *The Story of the Milky Way: A Cherokee Tale,* a 1995 *Scientific American* Young Readers Book Award winner. He lives in Greenfield Center, New York.

TERESA FLAVIN

is an American who lives in Scotland. She visited the U.S. to research the art in this book at the National Museum of the American Indian and other library collections. She is also the illustrator of *The Old Cotton Blues* by Linda England, and *Silver Rain Brown* by M. C. Helldorfer. She lives in Glasgow, Scotland.

The Center for the Collaborative Classroom (CCC) is a nonprofit organization dedicated to students' growth as critical thinkers who learn from, care for, and respect one another. Since 1980, we have created innovative curricula and provided continuous professional learning that empower teachers to transform classrooms, build school community, and inspire the academic and social growth of children.

Authentic literature is at the heart of our literacy programs. Children's books are deeply interwoven into every lesson, either in a read-aloud or as part of individual student work. Rich, multicultural fiction and nonfiction bring the full range of human experience and knowledge into the classroom, reinforce students' sense of belonging within it, and connect the classroom to the wider world.

Engaged teachers facilitate the exchange of student ideas in collaborative classrooms. These conversations spark curiosity and a desire to participate in the learning process that reap benefits far beyond the immediate goals of learning to read and write. Combining quality curricula and great literature enriches the educational experience for all students and teachers.

We would like to express our thanks to Penguin Young Readers Group for allowing us to reprint this book.